Infinite Echoes

Poems Inspired by God
Poems of Faith & Promises

Carolyn Duggins

Infinite Echoes | Carolyn Duggins

THERESA DANIEL — TDD Global Coaching and Leadership Group

Email: theresadnl@gmail.com
Website: https: theresaddaniel.com
609-280-2866

Dear Reader,

It is with great joy and heartfelt admiration that I introduce you to the inspiring collection of poetry by Pastor Carolyn Duggins. As a longtime friend and member of her family, I have had the privilege of witnessing firsthand the extraordinary compassion, leadership, and warmth that shine through in every line of her work.

Pastor Duggins' poetry is more than just words on a page; it is a testament to the power of faith, the resilience of the human spirit, and the transformative potential of love. Her words capture the essence of the Christian community in Philadelphia, embodying the very qualities of excellence, understanding, and unwavering support that define Pastor Duggins' own leadership.

Through her poetry, Pastor Duggins invites us to embark on a journey of self-discovery, healing, and growth. Her verses serve as gentle reminders of our inherent worth and potential, inspiring us to embrace the challenges of life with courage and hope.

As I read through this collection, I was reminded of the countless lives that have been touched and transformed by Pastor Duggins' ministry. Her words have a way of piercing the soul, awakening us to the presence of God in our everyday lives, and nudging us closer to our highest selves in HIM.

Whether you are a longtime member of Pastor Duggins' congregation, a fellow poet seeking inspiration, or simply someone in need of a little light and hope, I urge you to open your heart and mind to the wisdom and beauty contained within these pages.

Pastor Duggins' poetry is a gift – a gift to her community, to the body of Christ, and to all who are fortunate enough to encounter her words. It is my sincere hope that this collection will reach far and wide, touching lives and spreading the message of love, compassion, and understanding that is at the heart of Pastor Duggins' ministry.

With deepest respect and admiration,

Dr. Theresa D. Daniel

April 8. 2024

Dedication

To my sister, Wilhelmina Duggins
and
My nephew, Tracey Wiliam J. Duggins

In memory of my loving parents:
Pastor William Duggins
and
Shepherd Mother Annie L. Duggins

Acknowledgements

To my Lord and Savior Jesus Christ:
I praise You with all my heart. I can never fully express the love I have for You. I am so grateful for Your eternal grace, mercy, love, and faithfulness. Thank You for choosing me that I may give You the glory.

To my nephew Tracey William J. Duggins:
Thank you so much for being there. You may not realize how I appreciate all that you do. Thank you for your love, support, and encouragement. Love you.

To Pastor Rodney Roberson and my Kingdom Empowerment Ministries Family:
I am forever grateful to God for you. Thank you for showing me your love and support.

To my Garden of Prayer Memorial Center Family:
Thank you for being the beginning of my journey. Thank God for all of you too numerous to name personally. I am grateful to God for you.

In Memoriam of those forever present in our heart...

My mother: Annie L. Duggins

Mom, I am ever grateful that the Lord chose you to be my loving mother. You lived as an example of holiness, grace, love, and strength. I have always treasured your compassion and godly advice. You always encouraged me to do my best. Thank you for teaching me to trust in God and rely on your favorite scripture in Daniel 3:4 *"Our God Is able."* I miss you so much. You will always be a treasure in my heart.

My father: William Duggins

Daddy, you know I have always said that I could not have chosen better parents than you and mom. Being a PK (preacher's kid) made me who I am. Your love and protection made me feel that I never had to fear because you were always there to support me. I miss listening to you preach and teach at church and at home. Thank you for teaching me the foundation of prayer and God's Word. I miss you and treasure the legacy you are. I am proud to be your daughter.

My sister: Wilhelmina Duggins

Many people thought we looked alike and we were twins. Though we weren't twins, I was honored when everyone asked, "Are you twins?" We grew up together with love and respect for each other.

Growing up we sang in the choir, but I fondly remember you and I singing a cappella together at church and at home. We had an unbreakable bond. Thank you for always encouraging me and being my inspiration. Always my sister/my friend.

Author's Note:
Why I write poems...

To my dear readers,

Picture this: a young girl curled up with her worn, beloved Bible, its pages yellowed and soft with age. That little girl is me; that old Bible is a treasure trove of memories. It's where I first discovered the power of God's Word to comfort, inspire, and guide me.

You see, I grew up in a home where faith was woven into the very fabric of our lives. My parents and pastors poured their hearts into teaching me about the love of Jesus. I wanted to find a way to express my gratitude for their sacrifice and their profound impact on my soul.

That's when writing poems began to flow from my heart. Poems are heartfelt expressions of worship, reflections on God's Word, and words of encouragement for those I love most. I poured my soul onto the page, penning verses for special services at our church, for Pastoral Anniversaries, Church Anniversaries, and Appreciation Services.

Looking back, I realize that writing was my way of joining my voice to the chorus of praise that rose from my heart. It was a sacred act of worship, a way to lift the name of Jesus and share the hope that burned within me.

Through the years, as I read and studied God's Word, I fell in love with the poetic beauty of Scripture. The books of Job, Psalms, Proverbs, and Song of Solomon became my favorites, their lyrical language and profound truths resonating deep within my spirit.

I wrote poems to comfort my parents and sister and encourage them in the vital work God called them to do. Those words of love and appreciation were a balm to my soul, even as I longed to see them published in a book.

Now, that dream has finally come to fruition. Writing and completing this book has been a journey of joy and healing for me. Though my parents and sister are now with the Lord, I know they would be overjoyed to see their daughter's/sister's words of faith and encouragement shared with the world.

As you read these poems, I pray they will touch your heart and lift your spirit. May they remind you of God's unending love and a source of strength and hope for your journey.

Writing has been my way of saying "Thank you" to God for the incredible gift of His Word and the privilege of sharing it with others. It has been a joy and a blessing beyond measure.

So, I invite you now, dear reader, to open your heart and mind to the following words. Embrace the message of hope and love that is woven throughout these pages, and let writing be your sacred act of worship; a way to express your most profound faith and touch the lives of those around you.

For it is through our words that we can reflect the light of Christ into the world. And in doing so, we find our hearts set ablaze with the love of God.

With gratitude and love,

Pastor Carolyn

*"The difference between school and life?
In school, you're taught a lesson and then
given a test. In life, you're given a test that
teaches you a lesson."*

-Tom Bodett

Joy Filled Memories from the Heart

Table of Contents

I. Poems for Father

II. Poems for Mother

III. God's Woman

IV. Pastor. God's Instrument

V. Journey With Jesus

VI. When You Pray

VII. Be Encouraged

VIII. A Friend In Music

Poems for Father

In Memory of Elder William Duggins
By Evang. Carolyn Duggins
(2010)

*"See how great a love the father has
bestowed on us,
That we would be called children of God;
and such we are..."*

1 John 3:1 (NAS)

A Tribute to Fathers

A father is...
... a gift from God
He guides the road we trod,
He's there to lend a helping hand
A source of strength to help you stand.

... a gift from God
Head of the family,
To advise you and correct you
To show the way you can't see.

... a gift from God
His voice so firm and strong
Resounds to us his matchless love
Like a precious song.

Yes, a father is a gift from God
A friend throughout life's days.
He is our true example
To Him we now give praise.

(June 15, 1980)

Carolyn Duggins

Our Father

The greatest of all fathers
Is God our Heavenly One,
Who sent Jesus here to be our guide
... His only begotten Son

By giving of Himself so freely
God let us know He is near,
If we would only open our hearts
To His Son so precious and dear.

He promised to be our comfort
When all around seems dim,
All He asks is that we would
Have faith and confidence in Him.

Our Father has the world
Right in the palm of His hand,
He sees and He knows everything
Yes, He still controls the land.

Hold to God's unchanging hand
No matter what you must face,
His love will give to you the power
To rest in His matchless grace.

(June 21, 1981)

My Father

Just to know my father's there
... to comfort and scold
He's my example while I'm young
And as the years unfold

He lovingly gives so much of himself
Always helping me to see
The best God has in His storehouse
Waiting to give it to me.

His strong and courageous manner
Can comfort my saddened heart
When life's trials begin to face me
He says from God I must never depart.

He always knows the right words to say
To encourage and lift my soul
Through the journey along the highway
As I'm conformed to God's precious mold.

Just to know my father's there
Means so much to me
As I follow in his footsteps
With Jesus I can live eternally.

(June 21, 1981)

Carolyn Duggins

Our Father's Care

The greatest of all peace
Is in our Father's care
His love will never cease
He promises to always be there.

He'll always be your friend
Bringing you comfort untold.
Happiness and peace He'll send
Our Father's love is more precious than gold.

It is our Father's pleasure
To give to us the kingdom.
Rich blessings more than measure
Eternal life and freedom.

Every good and perfect gift
On all He freely bestows
To every heart He'll give a lift
For each of His children our Father knows.

(June 20, 1982)

I Shall See Him

Though I have never seen Him,
He watches o'er me each day
Though I have never seen Him.
He hears me when I pray,
Though I have never seen Him.
He answers to my call
Though I have never seen Him,
He will not let me fall.

I long to see my Savior
To see His nail-scarred side,
I long to see my Savior
'Twas for me He died
I long to see my Savior
It will mean so much to me
I long to see my Savior
Through all eternity.

One day and I shall see Him
Behold Him as He is
One day and I shall see Him
For I know that He yet lives;
One day I shall see Him
His face I'll surely greet
One day I shall see Him
Worship with the angels at His feet.
(June 19, 1983)

Carolyn Duggins

In His Hands

All of the earth's richest treasures
Are in my Father's hands
All that I need He supplies
He holds the world at His command.

Trusting in God's loving care,
I know that He surely will guide.
None other on Earth can compare
With my Father in whom I abide.

We walk and we talk together.
All along this journey through.
I stand in the strength of my Father,
All things through Him I can do.

He speaks to me words full of promise
If I follow His holy commands,
Blessings and power and all like this
Are in my Father's hands.

(June 19, 1983)

Our Father's Promise

Our Father has given a promise
Of a home He has prepared;
Filled with His glorious presence
With none other to be compared.

For His children a mansion awaits in heaven
An eternal place for the soul;
To live with Him forever,
A place where we'll never grow old.

Until then He watches o'er us
Protects us from all harm;
Our shelter and our refuge
Is in His loving arms.

Through the storms and billows
Upon life's rolling sea;
He's there to be our Shepherd
To give us sure victory.

Our Father carries us through all times
Amidst a world of strife;
With peace and joy in knowing
In Him we have eternal life.
(June 1984)

Carolyn Duggins

A Father's Day Tribute

*It's not a stature large or small
That merits you the praise;
But your kind and loving words
Your strong, yet gentle ways.*

*A creation of God's master plan
The pillar of the family;
In the image of our Heavenly Father,
The strength of our eternity.*

*We lean upon your support
To encourage when life's problem we face;
Telling us we can make it
Because of the Master's grace.*

*To you we give this tribute
You are so deserving of,
Written to say thank you,
To you with love*

(June 17, 1984)

Tribute to My Father

Matchless is the love I have for my father
For his wisdom and tender care
That I have found in none other.

He speaks words to encourage me
When life's trials I must face;
He lets me know I can make it with God
If I stay in the race.

Then there are some times
When I depend on his advice;
In the times of going through
And I must pay the price.

He teaches me to live right,
Always to be strong;
Then God will be the one,
To fight every wrong.

I'm thankful for my father,
For all he is to me;
The finest truest example
As the head of my family.

(June 16, 1985)

Carolyn Duggins

Walking With My Father

I look to my Heavenly Father,
He provides my every need;
As I daily follow
His safe and gentle lead.

Sometimes the road I travel
Is dark and seems no end;
But my Father is always there
For He is my truest friend.

I can trust in the shadow
Of His mighty wings;
And cast my cares upon Him.
In faith to Him I cling.

For I've found none other like Him,
As I journey through this land;
None other will go with me,
And hold on to my hand.

The Word of God has promised
There's joy beyond compare;
Walking with my Heavenly Father
Who'll go with me everywhere.

(June 21, 1987)

In His Image

Man was created in God's own image,
To be an example of strength in God;
Always obeying the voice of the Holy One
Wherever in life's pathway he trod.

But in search for his own wisdom
Man erred from the Divine plan;
Then the judgment from God came
And the curse upon mankind began.

God did not leave man alone
To remain with no hope for his end;
He sent His only Son, Jesus
To be a Savior and his friend.

His life He surely gave
To show His great love for all men;
So that one day we will see Him
Restored to His image again.

(June 19, 1988)

Carolyn Duggins

To My Heavenly Father

I give thanks to my Heavenly Father
For His daily watch over me;
For His arms of Divine protection,
In Him I have the victory.

He told me to cast upon Him all my burdens
As I look to Him in prayer;
He said He would guide my every step,
And He'd be with me everywhere.

Daily He loadeth me with blessings
His peace and love dwells within;
Lifting me through each day,
Knowing He has washed away my sin.

It is with these words I give Him glory
And magnify His dear name in praise;
As I give thanks to my Heavenly Father,
Through the length of my days.

(June 19, 1988)

A Holy Man

Dedicate thyself to Him
As God's holy man;
Shew forth unto the nation
The fulfillment of God's plan.

As a leader of the family,
In Him you must abide;
For your Heavenly Father
Is there to be your guide.

Thou art called for an example,
In spite of the great enemy;
Whose purpose is to destroy
God's perfect family

Be steadfast in God's plan
Honor Him and always pray;
With your eye upon the greatest Father
Acknowledge Him in this day.

(June 1989)

Carolyn Duggins

My Father's Reply

Upon my Heavenly Father I call,
For He is always near;
There, my protection as I walk
He cast away my every fear.

In Him is all the strength I need
To lead me all the way,
Until I reach the blessed home
He promised me in that day.

No more, then, shall I fear
Though evil around me draws nigh;
My ears await the loving voice
Of my dear Savior's reply

Well done, then shall I hear Him say,
I'll give thanks for His matchless grace;
And for all the hopes given to me
To endure and finish this race.

(June 18, 1989)

Your Light

The world needs your light
It must shine every day;
Keep following after Jesus
So others may see the way.

Faith will keep you going on
Even when the path is dim,
Never lose sight of the victory
You've already won in Him.

(June 17, 1990)

Carolyn Duggins

God's Love

In God's love,
There is gentleness of His special care,
Yet, in His great love
Is the strength of His presence
With us everywhere.

Sometimes we pause and think
Of His miraculous power.
And how, o'er all he watches
And nourishes the tiniest flower.

Though it is not given that we know,
Just how He does it all,
Our prayer of thanks should always be
For all things great and small.

(June 17, 1990)

With Special Thanks, Father

More than the words of thanks you I give
Father, you deserve the very best;
But in my way I want you to know
You stand above the rest.

Through your life you taught me
How to follow what is right;
And how to keep the standard within
That shines as a pure light.

You taught me how to trust in God
So I could walk in His Holy way;
But more than all of these things, father
I'm glad you taught me how to always pray.

Carolyn Duggins

No Greater Joy

I have found no greater joy
Than meeting my Father in prayer;
Never has there been a time
I found that He was not there.

With His open arms, He takes my cares
Then He fills me with inner peace;
And in the showers of His abundant mercy
I find that all my worries ceases

There my petitions are made known,
He says to my soul, " Be still";
Then He leads me as His dear child
In the comfort of His will.

No earthly joy can ever match,
Sweet communion at my Father's throne;
And in His great love I now live
Assured that I am never alone.

My Faithful Father

How faithful Thou hast been, dear Father
You support me through every;
For this and many reasons
I rejoice as I walk in Your way.

With Your loving arms outstretched
Your hands reached out to me;
And lifted me from the cares of the earth
When you sent your Son to set me free.

Of all Thy goodness, dear Father
No words could ever tell;
But with my praise to Thee, I want you to know
In your presence I want ever to dwell.

(June 21, 1992)

Carolyn Duggins

Joy In My Father's House

Blessed are the thoughts of delight
Of being in God's presence by His side;
My thoughts turn to heaven called home,
Where His love and peace ever abide.

Now in my ear I hear His voice echo
"Come unto me and rest;
He invites me to that royal feast,
There to sit and His feet and be blessed.

Where no more the cares of life to fear
In Thy mansion where this world is left behind;
There no more to shed a tear,
Only the joy in my Savior I'll find.

For in the blessed home of God
Unspeakable joy is awaiting;
As I gather with the angelic host,
My everlasting songs of victory there will be ringing.

(June 20, 1993)

Poems for Mother

In Memory of Mother Annie Duggins
By Evang. Carolyn Duggins
(2010)

*"Her children rise up and call her blessed;
Her husband also, and he praises her.
Many women have done excellently,
but you surpass them all..."*
Proverbs 31: 28-31

Carolyn Duggins

Thoughts of Mother

When I think of Mother
And the life that she lives,
It always comes to my mind
All the love she freely gives

There's a spirit of unselfish sharing
For which she is well known,
Among all who have met her
With care the seed of love is sown.

On the joy of her smile we depend
To give us hope and cheer,
And her rich advice guides us
Turning away our fear.

Mother, you have made the difference
By reaching out your hand,
And as you pray for all your children
By faith, we learn to stand.

Gifts of Love – A Christian Mother

O gift of love, our God has given,
A mother of hope, filled with grace and wisdom.
Thou art to us a precious treasure,
For the joy you give in unspeakable measure.
You have been to us an inspiring one,
Strong in faith knowing with Jesus it can be done.
Never wavering, nor in doubt or fear
Looking to Jesus who's always near
Your life you freely and willingly share
Patiently loving, showing that you care.
Listening to His divine call,
O what love you have given to all.
Your voice resounding in the strength of faith.
Increasing our hope in His matchless grace.
Used by God where'er you be,
Spreading the message of peace and victory.
O gift of love, our God has given
A mother of hope, filled with grace and wisdom
We'll ne'er forget how you taught us to pray
And live for Jesus day by day.

God's Woman

In Memory of Mother Annie Duggins
By Evang. Carolyn Duggins
(2010)

"God's comfort is like a mother's comfort."
Isaiah 66:13

A Christian Woman

There are many types of women
That travel through this land,
This was all a part
Of Gods creative plan.

God saw the need to have
Someone to walk by man's side,
So He made a woman
With whom man could confide.

Appointed as man's helpmeet
As the Word of God commands,
She is to him a source of love
To encourage him to stand.

Her beauty is far deeper
Than the eye can see,
Especially those in whom
our Savior dwells
And shines radiantly.

She is His glorious handiwork
Formed by His own hands,
Full of grace and knowledge
With wisdom to understand.

No matter how great the task
Or small a problem may be,
She's always there to comfort

Carolyn Duggins

And bids our worries flee,

Christian woman, you're a beacon
For all the world to view
An example you are to all
Who follow after you.

(June 28, 1981)

God's Woman

A woman of beauty
Our God created for man,
Through it is a mystery
From his side she began

She came as man's companion
God's purpose to fulfill,
Endowed with God's compassion
Love, comfort and goodwill.

A woman clothed
In strength and majesty,
With good works she is robed
She sits not idly.

Her life reflects
The grace and glory of heaven,
She is God's elect
She is God's woman.

(June 27, 1982)

Carolyn Duggins

Holy Women

No price can be placed on her worth,
She is more precious than silver or gold;
Just glance throughout all the earth,
You'll find a woman of beauty to behold.

Created for the man's glory .
Holy, with Christ living inside;
'Twas God's plan in the creation story,
For the woman and man to abide.

Sharing the gift of God's love,
Holy in heart and in mind;
She's gentle and sweet as a dove,
Living in God's holy design.

Behold the beauty of holy women,
Her wisdom and knowledge to share;
She's more than the rarest of gems,
Her glory shines everywhere.

Though sometimes she's standing alone
Holding forth God's holy light;
One day she shall sit 'round the throne,
An example of His royal delight

(June 26, 1983)

God-Made Woman

I know that God made thee,
Holy women everywhere;
Molded rich in beauty,
A life with man to share.

You're a treasure that's so precious,
A jewel through all the earth;
God's adorned you with His presence,
You are Royal from your birth.

Your name He's called woman,
Then He placed you in the garden;
Clothed you with His Holiness,
And called you to be a helpmeet to men.

Your days we cannot number,
Your life He does unfold;
Planned by the Holy Saviour,
From your youth through days untold.

You're aglow with His radiance,
Godly, holy and divine;
One day and you shall hear Him say,
I'm glad that you are mine.

(June 24, 1984)

Carolyn Duggins

Woman, God's Creation

When God made a woman
He arranged her in holy beauty,
To stand by the man
Faithful to her duty.

Her light was made to shine
Proud to be the one,
That God has ordained and chosen
For the indwelling of His Son.

He gave her love and wisdom
Kindness and a smile,
To share with those around her
Men, women, and the little child.

He made her an example
Of His holiness,
That every eye beholds her
In purity and righteousness.

When God made a woman
He made her as a fine treasure,
Worthy to be His beloved
To be cherished beyond measure.

(June 23, 1985)

God's Plan for Woman

Holding to the principles of pure righteousness,
God's woman bears a mark of Divine holiness;
Beautified with His salvation,
She stands for Him alone,
Clothed in the royal robe
Given by God on His throne.

To all who behold her,
She exhibits faith and loyalty.
As the bride to her groom, she vows fidelity;
True to one whose love divine
Draws her unto Him,
Gently He leads her every step,
No path is lonely or dim.

Through this dark world
She's an ambassador of God's love,
Giving others some sunshine,
With gentleness of a dove;
Her words in meekness are spoken,
But Jesus' standards she must hold,
Standing forth as a lion, a witness firm and bold.

Women of God must ever hold
The mighty hand of God,
Never doubting but ever keeping
God's principles o'er the path you trod;
God made woman in His image,
To be a help unto man,
To fulfill the work He has assigned
from the Master plan.

(June 22, 1986)

Carolyn Duggins

Woman of God

Woman of God--- creation
From Gods' master plan;
Thou art a vessel of beauty
Given unto man.

Thou wearest a robe of righteousness
Dressed in royal array,
Clothed with His divine purity
As a light for the world today.

The charge of holiness is upon thee
Thy covenant thou must keep,
Living daily for Jesus
The harvest thou must reap.

Souls awaiting deliverance
Are won through your holy life,
That bids them to the Savior
The hope of eternal life.

One day the crown of victory
Will be yours to wear,
When to His charge you've been faithful
As a witness unto God everywhere.

(June 28, 1987)

God's Charge

Holiness unto the Lord
Is God's charge to you;
Separated from all sin
Faithful to God and true.

To Him yield all allegiance
Stand always for the right;
He's ever standing with you;
Your battles He will fight.

Take courage, for He is faithful
His Word will never fail;
Just keep your eyes upon Jesus
He's mighty to prevail.

The victory's in holding on
Put your trust in His powerful hand;
Never doubt and never worry
For surely He's in command.

Just listen to His gentle voice
Saying to thy soul, be still;
For there's a reward that awaits
Those who live in His perfect will.

(June 28, 1987)

Carolyn Duggins

God's Chosen Women

The holiness that shines
From God's chosen women,
Has a special glow of new life
Of the hope that Jesus has given.

Aglow with God's anointing
She lifts His praises high.
A joyful witness of His love
Against the ways of sin she does cry.

Standing steadfast in His righteousness
Obedient to His Word,
Strong in His faith without wavering
Holding the Gospel of Peace as her sword.

For God has endowed her with special beauty
As a light for the world to see,
The redeeming work that all began
Through Jesus at Calvary.

(June 26, 1988)

The Blessed Woman

Holy woman – thou art called blessed
Chosen by the richness of His grace,
Endowed with God's wondrous beauty
That is aglow upon thy Holy face.

Holy woman – thou art called blessed
Redeemed from the stain of sin,
For the hope of your salvation comes
Through Christ who lives within.

For God has found thee worthy
As a vessel of honor for His praise
He has made of you a precious jewel
To live for Him always.

Holy woman – thou art called blessed
One day His full blessings He'll unfold
When you stand in the glorious presence of God
And His loving face you'll behold.

(June 25, 1989)

Carolyn Duggins

The Holy Standard

Lift up the Holy standard
Keep living Holy every day;
If in God you always stand,
His voice only shall you obey.

For He made you a Holy creation
In the beauty of Holiness like Him;
A precious work of His mighty hands
To be a light for a world that is dim.

Keep all of God's Holy commandments
And tell of His grace through your days;
For Christ is soon to appear
And receive all who acknowledge His ways.

Lift up His Holy standard
Let Him in you ever abide;
And rejoice in the hope of life eternal
With the God of all comfort as your guide.

(June 25, 1989)

A Chosen Epistle

Woman, how beautiful is thy creation,
A wonder of life you are;
Uniquely designed by God's hand
To shine as His radiant star.

Walk in the beauty of holiness,
Let Him take your hand every day;
Ask of Him to learn of His humility
As you walk in His loving way.

Be a storehouse of His wisdom,
Teach others through words and deeds;
Then the tender souls who follow after
Will have a living epistle to read.

When you think of all God's treasures,
And the blessings bestowed upon you;
Rejoice! As God's woman you are chosen
Worthy of His Spirit dwelling in you.

(June 25, 1989)

Carolyn Duggins

I Must Work

Keep working till thy work is done
Until the Lord says it's enough;
Undeterred by the roads ahead
Even when the way gets rough.

For there is a crown awaiting
Prepared by God for thee;
But it's only yours if you press on
And you'll have the victory.

Whatever He has chosen for you
Do it with all your might;
Then your testimony will be when
He comes; 'I fought a good fight.'

(June 25, 1989)

God's Chosen Bride

How fearfully and wonderfully made
From the rib of Adam's side;
Woman was God's choice to be
United with man as his bride.

***He** clothed her with rich beauty within*
Unseen by the natural eye;
Then crowned her with His royal love,
From His bright realm on high.

He robed her in His Spirit
And joined her with man to follow His Holy Will;
That by a faithful walk in Him
Every promise He would fulfill.

God's invitation is to a home in Heaven
For His covenant through Jesus, still stands secure.
Every creation adorned in His love
Can join with the bridegroom ever more.

(June 27, 1993)

Pastor, God's Instrument

In Memory of Elder William Duggins
By Evang. Carolyn Duggins
(2010)

"And I will give you pastors according to mine heart, which shall feed you with knowledge and understanding."
Jeremiah 3:15

Lord, Use Me

As each busy day begins
I pray to know God's will
Because I know God knows what is best;
I go to Him while all is calm and still.

My prayer is that He use me
As an instrument in His hand,
That I may tell of His love and promises
As the foundation on which all can stand.

In the silence of that special place
Dedicated for my quiet devotion,
It is there I find the Holy One
And behold His Holy Son.

The presence of God's joy surrounds me
And He bids me to meet with Him there,
To feel His great power and direction
Down at the altar of prayer.

-Evang. Carolyn Duggins

Carolyn Duggins

God's Call to His Servant

God called him to preach His Word
To be instant in and out of season,
That God's message would be heard
Of God's promise with man to reason.

As His servant he would open his mouth
And God's Word would freely flow
To His people of the north, east, west and south,
And upon them His blessings He'd bestow.

He must dedicate himself to Him
And heed the Master's call;
Though the road he travels may be sometimes dim
God will never let him fall.

If for Him he would firmly stand
In His vineyard toil and labor
And follow God's Holy command
In His sight he would find favor.

His voice will say, "Well done,
Thou good and faithful servant."
This battle for souls has been won
Welcome to a land that's good and pleasant.
(October 1984)

-Evang. Carolyn Duggins

For Such A Time As This

Called from the world of sin
For such a time as this,
To a Holy life of joy within
With love and peaceful bliss.

Chosen to be a Shepherd
In this land that God gave,
Telling all of God's Word
For a dying world to save

Raised as a mighty leader,
An example of the Holy One;
To be God's anointed preacher
An ambassador of God's Son.

Prepared he walks among us,
He stands on God's Holy promise.
As a servant of the Righteous
For such a time as this.
(October 1983)

-Evang. Carolyn Duggins

Carolyn Duggins

Our Shepherd Teaches

Who is the one who teaches us the way that's right?
To follow the path of Jesus every day and night?

His voice so loud and strong
Against the snares of sin;
Who beckons us to seek Jesus
And let the Saviour in?

Who admonishes us to daily read
God's Word and pray?
That we may stand so firmly in this last day...

None other but our shepherd,
The watchman of our soul,
Preaches the true and living Word
A message to the young and old

If we follow in His image of Jesus
God's only Son;
One day he'll receive his wage and
know the job is well done.
(October 1982)

-Evang. Carolyn Duggins

The Pastor's Message

*The message our pastor preaches
Is not new but old;
It's a witness and it teaches
Our Saviour's coming already foretold.*

*The words he speaks are given
Not from man or any story;
They are words full of wisdom
Inspired by God for his glory.*

*As a messenger of God,
He preaches to rescue the weak,
He prays that on the road we trod
Our loving Saviour we'll always seek.*

*As a good shepherd, he watches over
And tenderly cares for each soul
Leading the way to the Saviour
Feeding the lambs of the fold.*

*All we need to do is listen
And heed to God's messenger's call.
We shall receive the gift God's given
Freely to one and all.*

*His message repeats the example
He sets before us each day
Holding the light of the Saviour
Teaching us to watch and pray.*
(October 1981)

-Evang. Carolyn Duggins

Carolyn Duggins

Our Pastor

Our pastor is a watchman placed upon the wall
Daily praying and travailing for God's people
One and all.

He holds a light to guide us amidst the troubled land;
For Jesus' coming is at hand.

Our pastor speaks in wisdom as given him by God,
The message of the gospel where'er his feet may trod.

Being guided by God's Spirit,
He preaches whether many or few.
To herald glad tiding of hope in the
land through and through.

Our pastor is our counselor
when all seems lost in despair.
Encouraging us that Jesus loves us and He cares.

His voice echoes of holiness
as taught by God's own Word.
O what peace it brings to many
Wherever this message is heard.

If we follow our pastor's example
as he does the work of God,
Standing up for Jesus,
Our feet with gospel shod.

Infinite Echoes

If we do as God commands,
How happy we will be.
One day when life is over
Jesus' face we'll surely see.
(October 1980)

-Evang. Carolyn Duggins

Carolyn Duggins

God's Special Person

God has some special people
Whom He can freely use,
For these are available vessels
Who are not ashamed to tell His good news.

God makes choice of these ambassadors
Through whom His message can be heard;
These He calls to preach, live and to pray
As He empowers them by His Word.

These glorify Him as obedient servants
Never failing to heed God's call;
Great or small – whatever the task
They must be ready to give God their all.

God raised up among us such a special person
A humble man, yet he had wisdom
that meant so much;
And all who came to know him
Were witnesses of the power of God's touch.

To all whose lives his ministry touched, "Hold fast."
For the principles he taught us we must never lose,
Let us strive to follow on in his steps
Because it will be hard to fill his shoes.

-Evang. Carolyn Duggins (1995)

What Profit A Man

In this day of modern and new ideas
Many questions often arise;
Men search to know "where is God?"
And ask if He's somewhere in the sky?

Through the gain of earthly goods
The answer is sometimes sought;
With hearts far from God's command
That His Holy Word has taught.

The voice of God's servant echoes,
"Arise, come one and all to pray.
For the abundance of His blessings awaits
To all who draw near Him and obey."

What profit a man to have wealth untold
And gain all of the world's pleasures?
Then to find one day that all is lost,
And to have missed all of eternity's treasures.

-Evang. Carolyn Duggins

Carolyn Duggins

A Holy Man

Dedicate thyself to Him
As God's holy man;
Shew forth unto the nation
The fulfillment of God's plan.

As a leader of the family,
Strong in him abide;
For your Heavenly Father
Is there to be your guide.

Thou art called for an example
In spite of the great enemy;
His purpose is to destroy
God's perfect family.

Be steadfast in God's plan,
Honor Him and always pray.
With your eye upon the greatest Father
Acknowledge Him in this day.

-Evang. Carolyn Duggins

Journey With Jesus

Let this mind be in you, which was also in Christ Jesus. Who, being in the form of God, thought it not robbery to be equal with God: But made himself of no reputation, and took upon him the form of a servant, and was made in the likeness of men: And being found in fashion as a man, he humbled himself, and became obedient unto death, even the death of the cross.
Philippians 2:5-8 (KJV)

Carolyn Duggins

What Manner of Man

Through the years our thoughts reflect
Of a unique man of royal birth.
His life, in a short span of time
Wrought a change to the earth.

Freely He came with eternal life,
For all that behold God's plan;
Yet from Him many oft turn aside,
Refusing to accept this man.

Though despised and rejected,
His everlasting love
Flowed freely at the Cross;
There He bore sin's agony,
His will that no one suffer loss.

Rich In mercy and in love
He died at Calvary;
Rising, He paid salvation's cost,
Setting the captive free.

Behold His works, behold this man
From His Father, He is sent;
An example of enduring love
To all who will repent.

O Marvelous and wondrous gift
Giving to us unmerited favor;
What manner of man is this
Who came to be our Saviour?

The Words of Christ

Echoes of those words I hear
Jesus uttered at Calvary;
Stirring deep down within my heart,
My Saviour's great love for me.

Enduring the cross, even 'til death.
Ne'er shall I forget Him there alone;
Forsaken by man and crucified
Standing for my sin to atone.

Triumph o'er sin, death, hell and the grave
Was won by Him that day,
A ransom of poor dying souls.
A price none else could pay.

So much I owe for all He has done
The glory I give to His name;
I cherish the precious words He spoke
His praises forever proclaim.

Carolyn Duggins

For Me

The pain of sin and death He bore
Upon the rugged cross;
There He took my appointed place
With the guilty, condemned to eternal loss.

I owe so much unto Him
For the suffering He bore that day,
Surely the price of debt I owed
None else could ever pay.

Because of this, I'll ever give Him
Adoration and praise
Worshipping Him in my life
Rejoicing through the days.

I'll spread the news of my Savior's love
For this He was crucified
For I know that on that great day
Surely, it was for me He died.

-Evang. Carolyn Duggins

Never A Man Spoke Like This

Never a man spoke like this,
Can you hear His mighty voice?
He's beckoning to all the world
To **stop** and make a choice.

Behold His gift of love before us
Gives life abundant and free;
For He loosened the painful bond of death
Through His blood on Calvary.

The penalty of sin is waiting
Those who do not hear;
Hear the voice of Jesus who crieth
And bids you to draw near.

Do not fail to heed His voice
In mercy He is waiting today;
One day He will no longer call
Do not turn Him away.
(June 1998)

Carolyn Duggins

My Friend, Jesus

I know in whom I believe
Upon whom I can depend
There is none other than my Saviour Jesus
He is my friend.

Constantly He stands, bearing me up
When my strength is small;
Every day He fulfills His promises
He is my all and all.

With His watchful eye o'er me
My guide along the way;
His joy and strength He gives to me
Supplying all my needs day by day.

Through each cross I bear He strengthens me
I must never complain,
But I'll be stable.
Then in each victory I can say
The God I serve, "He is able!"
(March 1993)

-Evang. Carolyn Duggins

A Fulfilled Promise

If Jesus had not died,
Leaving His home above;
What if Jesus had not died,
How could we then know His love?

None o'er the earth was worthy.
To atone the course of man's sin;
For the glory of His Father, He died
And new life through Him was given.

Heirs through Jesus' precious blood
That flowed from His pierced side.
Can ever draw near to Him.
And in His love daily abide.

A promise was fulfilled,
When that redemptive work was done;
And the blessed joy of eternal life
Came through God's beloved Son.
(March 1991)

When you pray...

"Praying at all times in the Spirit, with all prayer and supplication. To that end, keep alert with all perseverance, making supplication for all the saints."
Ephesians 6:18 (ESV)

Precious Hours of Prayer

So precious are the hours,
Times spent alone with my Lord
In the secret of prayer I kneel to
Meditate upon His Holy Word.

There out of my heart I call upon Him
For it is He who answers my prayers;
There I seek to learn of His way
As I cast upon Him all my cares.

There the echoes of praise I lift up
Filling that sweet, quiet place;
Then God's goodness overshadows me
And I thank Him for His matchless grace.

So those precious hours in prayer
Are the delight of my soul each day;
In the glory of His presence I'll ever abide
And with Him I will always stay.

-Evang. Carolyn Duggins

Carolyn Duggins

In Prayer With Jesus

One day as I knelt down to pray
Jesus met me there.
My faith reached out and His voice I heard
Saying, "Cast upon Me all your care."

His gentle voice echoed in my ears
Though I had never looked upon His face.
Then the brightness of His presence shone
And His glory filled the place.

As I knelt with eyes closed, I opened my heart
And God's storehouse opened to let me in;
His loving arms assured me prayer was answered
And His work in me He would now begin.

With childlike delight, I hurry to meet Him,
To receive the pleasures of His direction;
Where my offerings of praise is to Him alone,
Christ, to whom I owe all my affection.

Since I hid His Word in the temple of my heart
And cried, "Lord, Thy will I'll obey."
How sweet the path He let me walk
And know He's the author of my every day.

-Evang Carolyn Duggins

My Hour of Prayer

*With lifted hands unto the Lord
Daily I seek His will;
Then as I pray He holds me fast
And gently says, "Be still."*

*Down on my knees He lifts me up
Onto a higher ground.
There I learn of His wonderful peace
And behold His mercy all around.*

*To unknown heights He carries me
Above the cares of this earthly throne.
Unto the glory of that heavenly place
Where joy unspeakable is ever known.*

*Everyday, somewhere I meet God in prayer
My voice I lift to the Holy One.
There on this lofty realm on high
I've found sweet communion with God's Son.*

-Evang. Carolyn Duggins

Carolyn Duggins

I Must Work

I must work for the time is near.
Behold my Savior soon shall appear.
Though the day of His coming is not known,
In His Word He has promised to come for His own.

I must work for the time will soon be
When Jesus shall return with the shout of victory.
All sorrows and toils, they shall all cease
In the coming day of the Prince of Peace.

I must work in His great harvest field
And to His will I must daily yield;
Wherever He leads me I promised to go
That seed of the gospel He may sow.

Unto Him who is precious I give my all,
And continue always obedient to His call.
Then I'll rejoice with one soul once lost but now found
Who has embraced a hope of that higher ground.

-Evang Carolyn Duggins

My Altar of Prayer

A refuge for my soul
Where I can cast every care;
The place where my Jesus awaits me
Is at my altar of prayer.

There I talk with my loving Savior
Who bids all of my burdens to flee;
In the quiet of His holy presence
He assures my victory.

Then the joy of the Lord fills me
With the hope that He is near.
I hush to the voice of my Savior
The one who conquers every fear.

Many are the blessings I receive
in that heavenly place;
There God strengthens me with His power
Through the sufficiency of His grace.

I will abide in that sweet, quiet place
For the anointing of the Holy One is there.
Where I love to magnify Jesus
At my altar of prayer.

-Evang. Carolyn Duggins

Carolyn Duggins

No Greater Joy

*I have found no greater joy
Than meeting my Father in prayer;
Never has there been a time
I found that He was not there.*

*With His open arms, He takes my cares
Then He fills me with inner peace;
And in the showers of His abundant mercy
I find that all my worries cease.*

*There my petitions are made known
He says to my soul, "Be still;"
Then He leads me as His dear child
In the comfort of His will.*

*No earthly joy can ever match...
Sweet communion at my Father's throne.
And in His great love I now live
Assured that I am never alone.*

-Evang. Carolyn Duggins

Be Encouraged

"I lift up my eyes to the hills. From where does my help come from? My help comes from the Lord, who made heaven and earth."
Psalm 121:1-2 (ESV)

Carolyn Duggins

What Jesus Gives

When it seems alone
That you must do the task,
You'll gain the strength that you need
If Jesus you will only ask.

Be mindful of His presence
He promised to always be near;
Look to Him for guidance
To comfort and to cheer.

Be faithful unto Jesus
To you He'll give a song;
A melody in your heart
To sing all the day long.

-Evang Carolyn Duggins

Steadfast in Jesus

Steadfast in Jesus
Yielded to My Saviour Divine;
Walking with Him always,
Assured that He is mine.

As a servant of Jesus,
I know He leads me by His hand
Obedient I am willing
To follow His command.

Wherever He guides me
Then faithful I'll be;
Doing the good pleasure
Of Him who loves me.

Steadfast in Jesus
I'll keep running this race;
Until He is pleased
And I'll see His blessed face.

-Evang Carolyn Duggins

Carolyn Duggins

Jesus Knows

Jesus knows the path I take
As I journey day by day.
He watches o'er me gently leading
As I earnestly pray.
He is my song, sword, and shield
Against a host of foes.
He is the source of my joy and strength
I can call on Him for He knows.
Jesus knows all about me
My life is yielded to Him,
I stand on the promise of His word
Through sometimes the road seems dim.
Jesus is there to light the way
I'll never walk alone.
As long as I stay with him
And proclaim Him as my own.
Jesus knows and cares for me
I'll lean on Him always,
Standing faithful everyday
Knowing that living for Jesus pays.

-Evang Carolyn Duggins

Following God

Where'er my Saviour leads me
Surely I must follow;
In His Holy footsteps
Onward through each tomorrow.

He promised He would hold me
In the palm of His hand,
Giving me the strength I need
To obey His every command.

The Holy Ghost is my teacher
God said He would be my guide,
Through every dark pathway
In Him I can always abide.

I need not fret or be weary
Whatever comes each day,
For He is always with me
I cannot lose my way.

Where'er my Saviour leads me
I'll delight to know He's there
Never will I have to walk alone
I'm protected through every snare.

Where'er my Saviour leads me
I can praise Him day and night
For the blessed assurance that
Only He will make everything alright.

-Evang. Carolyn Duggins

Carolyn Duggins

Committed to God

A life of total commitment
Unto the call of God;
Our Shepherd watches o'er our soul
With the Gospel of Peace his feet are shod.

A witness unto all who will follow
As He leads with gentle care;
Staying daily at the altar,
Committed to God in prayer.

He stands firmly on God's Word,
Preaching God's power over sin.
Proclaiming of life everlasting,
Once Jesus has entered in.

A life of total commitment
Devoted as a servant of God;
A holy and true example
Where'er in life he must trod.

-Evang. Carolyn Duggins

For the Master's Use

My life belongs to Jesus
The keeper of my soul;
I give Him all the praise
For He hath made me whole.

I was so lost and lonely
No rest on earth could I find
Then I met a Savior who bid me
To leave all my cares behind

My life now belongs to Jesus
For He paid the great ransom for me;
It was the price that was needed
To set my mind and soul free.

I will daily offer Him my vessel
To fill me with His Holy, Love Divine;
So that the presence of my precious Saviour
Will from me forever shine.

-Evang. Carolyn Duggins

Carolyn Duggins

The Days of Youth

The days of youth pass quickly
For they cannot always last;
For they are the threshold to mature life
Where we hold fond memories of the past.

How precious are the days of youth
Where there's joy beyond compare.
God grants each moment as a gift
Where we're free from every care.

In these growing days we learn
The value of the world around;
And draw from God's loving plan
And see His grace in us abound.

So from the days of youth come many lessons
But it is not ours to know what tomorrow will bring
But by His divine hand God teaches
He's the author of everything.

-Evang. Carolyn Duggins

A Life's Journey

Lo, many the years have passed
Along this journey you've trod
With Jesus as your Saviour
You've found the joy of walking with God.

While walking the straight and narrow
A path that leads you home,
Your mind's made up to serve Jesus
And from Him, no never to roam

Sharing the hope of His coming
With those that you meet day by day,
In prayer you've been watching and waiting
His sweet voice you hear and obey.

God has called you out of darkness
In His glorious light,
To witness with others of His goodness
Doing that which is pleasing in His sight.

And when the crowning Saviour is come,
And your story of life is told,
The angels will say you pressed onward to see Him
That you shall come forth as pure gold.

-Evang. Carolyn Duggins

A Friend In Music

In Memory of Sister Wilhelmina Duggins
By Evang. Carolyn Duggins
(2010)

"I thank my God upon every
remembrance of you.."
Philippians 1:3 (NKJV)

The Blessings of God's Talents

Every talent is a blessing
Of God's wisdom and design
For before birth our lives are fashioned
By Him who is divine.

He places within us gifts and talents
That are selected with His greatest care
And they are given because of His love
For His love is precious and rare.

Never busy your talent
But give Him all glory and praise;
For God will bless with every good gift
As you acknowledge Him in all your ways.

-Evang. Carolyn Duggins

Carolyn Duggins

Hymns of Praise

I love to hear the hymns of praise,
O sweet music to repeat
To ring through God's eternal days,
The joy of dance in my feet.

No sound cannot ever replace
The wondrous sounds of old,
Like songs telling of God's amazing grace
And the greatest story ever told

Can you hear the swelling chords
Played on the instruments?
They bring comfort to me through God's words
Calming the day's events.

Yes, I love to hear the songs of praise
O sweet music to repeat.
One day I'll join the angel's praise
Hallelujah! My Saviour I'll greet.

-Evang. Carolyn Duggins

Musical Sounds

Music is a sound heard at an early age,
A lullaby is sung to quiet us at an infant stage.

The years go on in life's journey,
Days of joy and sometimes grief
Lo, the sounds of music
Offer a tender, sweet relief.

So gentle and full of comfort
Its sounds we oft repeat.
There is a place sure the heart can find
A shelter of retreat.

Upon instruments and organs and with loud voices
We raise a soul full of thanksgiving to God
In adoration and praise.

-Evang Carolyn Duggins

Carolyn Duggins

Songs of Praise

The echoes of the music sweet,
How well I often recall
In unison with joy repeat
Our hearts in praise one and all

Each tone so smooth upon the ear
Strikes up the loudest praise,
Hallelujah to the Lamb so dear
Through all eternal days.

I love to hear the music
Resounding every chord,
Spreading the message that reflects Jesus,
Our Saviour and Lord.

O to hear the gospel sounds
Repeat the melody's refrain
Let it continue o'er the world abound
Until Jesus comes again.

-Evang Carolyn Duggins

A Song

Sing unto the Lord
Sing praise to His Holy name
Tell of the wondrous goodness
Of Jesus who's always the same.

Make melody in your heart
Though trials you must face
The song will give you joy
As you meditate upon His grace.

Play skillfully upon the instrument
A resonant and merry chord
Echoing the name of Jesus
Who is our Saviour and Lord.

Though hills you must climb
Amidst your travel of life's sea,
The sweetest melody of a song
Will give you the victory.

As you walk life's road
The path may seem very long
Just rejoice in your heart
For Jesus will give you a song.

-Evang Carolyn Duggins

Carolyn Duggins

W - Willing to help or aid no matter what the task may be
I – Interested and concerned about the work of God
L – Loving and faithful in pleasing God
H – Hoping for that day to see our Saviour's face
E – Enriched by God's blessings
L – Living the life God will be pleased with
M – Making time until that great day
I – Intending to be used by God
N – Never tiring from doing God's work
A – Always faithful

D – Doing what is expected without a frown
U – Upholding God's work
G – Grateful
G – Glad to be saved
I – In all things I will give thanks
N – Nothing is impossible for my God
S – Satisified with Jesus alone

(September 1980)

Quotes by J. Oswald Sanders

○ Faith enables the believing soul to treat the future as present and the invisible as seen.

○ Our problem is not too little time, but making better use of the time we have. Each of us has as much time as anyone else.

○ God is always at work, though we cannot see it, preparing people He has chosen for leadership. When the crisis comes, God fits His appointee into the place ordained for him.

○ There is no such thing as a self-made spiritual leader. He is able to influence others spiritually only because the Spirit is able to work in and through him to a greater degree than in those he leads.

Quotes by Warren W. Wiersbe

o Trusting God means thinking and acting according to God's Word in spite of circumstances, feelings or consequences.

o Nothing paralyzes our lives like the attitude that things can never change. We need to remind ourselves that God can change things. Outlook determines outcome. If we see only the problems, we will be defeated; but if we see the possibilities in the problems, we can have victory.

o People who walk by faith don't see obstacles; they see opportunities.

o He knows when we go into the storm, He watches over us in the storm, and He can bring us out of the storm when His purposes have been fulfilled.

References

Sanders, J. Oswald. "Top 25 Quotes by L. Oswald Sanders." Retrieved from: www.azquotes.com

Wiersbe, Warren. "Top 25 Quotes by Warren Wiersbe." Retrieved from: www.azquotes.com

About the Author

Pastor Carolyn Duggins is a dynamic faith leader and author who has dedicated her life to serving others through the power of God's Word. Born the younger of two children to the late Elder William and Mother Annie L. Duggins, she was raised in a devoted Christian family that instilled a deep love for ministry from an early age.

After earning her Bachelor of Science in Elementary Education from St. Joseph's University in Philadelphia, PA, Pastor Duggins pursued her calling by graduating from Manna Bible Institute. Her educational background and faith foundation prepared her for her distinguished career in ministry.

The power of influence can catalyze transformation, sparking a burning fire across generations. For Pastor Carolyn Duggins, this transformative power came from her parents, the late Elder William and Mother Annie L. Duggins, and her spiritual parents, the late Bishop Benjamin H. Dabney and Mother Elizabeth Juanita Dabney, of the Garden of Prayer.

Their unwavering faith and commitment to God's work were not just examples to follow; they were a spark that ignited

Carolyn's own calling and set her on the path of ministry, a path she now proudly continues to walk. She was licensed as an evangelist in 1970 under Elder William Duggins at the Garden of Prayer World Prayer Center.

Pastor Duggins has served with great passion and dedication at the Garden of Prayer Memorial Center since 1976. She faithfully served as an Assistant Pastor from 1995 to 2003 and has proudly led the congregation as Pastor since 2003. In addition to her leadership role at Garden of Prayer Memorial Center, she co-pastors Kingdom Empowerment Ministries, demonstrating her commitment to spreading the Word of God through multiple platforms.

Pastor Duggins is a multifaceted minister and intercessor of prayer, gifted in evangelism, teaching, singing, and writing. She has served as a Sunday School teacher, Bible Institute teacher, VBS teacher, and choir director, using her diverse talents to uplift others and spread the gospel. Her love of writing and poetry emerged from her years of ministry, leading her to co-authoring the book "Voices of Grace" with Apostle Julia McKinley.

Throughout her life and ministry, Pastor Duggins has learned the profound importance of knowing God, hearing His voice, understanding His power, and discerning His call. She embodies the wisdom gained from a lifetime of walking with Him and sharing His love with others.

www.ingramcontent.com/pod-product-compliance
Lightning Source LLC
Chambersburg PA
CBHW020325130626
46549CB00003B/1022